INSIDE MODERN CITIES

PROVIDING
WASTE SOLUTIONS
FOR A CITY

BY YVETTE LaPIERRE

CONTENT CONSULTANT
Stephanie C. Bolyard, PhD
Environmental Engineer

Core Library

An Imprint of Abdo Publishing
abdopublishing.com

Cover image: Waste collectors help remove and
dispose of a community's waste.

abdopublishing.com

Published by Abdo Publishing, a division of ABDO, PO Box 398166,
Minneapolis, Minnesota 55439. Copyright © 2019 by Abdo Consulting
Group, Inc. International copyrights reserved in all countries. No part of this
book may be reproduced in any form without written permission from the
publisher. Core Library™ is a trademark and logo of Abdo Publishing.

Printed in the United States of America, North Mankato, Minnesota
022018
092018

THIS BOOK CONTAINS
RECYCLED MATERIALS

Cover Photo: People Images/iStockphoto
Interior Photos: People Images/iStockphoto, 1; Seth Wenig/AP Images, 4–5; iStockphoto, 7;
Red Line Editorial, 9, 37; Wagner Santos/Photoshot/Newscom, 12–13; Francesco de Marco/
Shutterstock Images, 16; Herman Bustamante Jr./Contra Costa Times/Newscom, 19; Stefan
Puchner/picture-alliance/dpa/AP Images, 22–23; Matthias Balk/dpa/picture-alliance/Newscom,
26–27; Caro Photo Agency/Claudia Hechtenberg/Newscom, 30; Francis Joseph Dean/Deanpictures/
Newscom, 32–33, 43; Laura Greene/The High Point Enterprise/AP Images, 35; Jill Toyoshiba/MCT/
Newscom, 38, 45

Editor: Maddie Spalding
Imprint Designer: Maggie Villaume
Series Design Direction: Claire Vanden Branden

Library of Congress Control Number: 2017962645

Publisher's Cataloging-in-Publication Data

Names: LePierre, Yvette, author.
Title: Providing waste solutions for a city / by Yvette LaPierre.
Description: Minneapolis, Minnesota : Abdo Publishing, 2019. | Series: Inside modern cities |
    Includes online resources and index.
Identifiers: ISBN 9781532114847 (lib.bdg.) | ISBN 9781532154676 (ebook)
Subjects: LCSH: Engineering design--Juvenile literature. | Sanitation--Juvenile literature. |
    City planning--Juvenile literature. | Cities and towns--Juvenile literature. | Refuse and
    refuse disposal--Juvenile literature.
Classification: DDC 624.023--dc23

CONTENTS

ALL ABOUT WASTE

F resh Kills Landfill in New York City, New York, was once the world's largest landfill. It operated from 1948 to 2001. At the height of its operation, New Yorkers dumped approximately 29,000 tons (26,300 metric tons) of waste into the landfill each day. But today government workers are turning the former landfill into a park. Workers covered the waste with layers of soil and other materials. Decaying waste releases gases, such as methane. These gases can be harmful to the environment. Strong fabrics and plastic netting absorb the gas so it doesn't reach the surface.

Freshkills Park, the site of the former Fresh Kills Landfill, is now a wildlife habitat and public park.

They also protect the environment from leachate. Rainwater can pick up compounds such as metals from waste. This contaminated liquid is leachate. A system of pipes moves rainwater away from the soil layers. This prevents rain from eroding the soil on top of the waste. The top layer is made up of planting soil. Plants grow roots, which further stabilize the mounds. Freshkills Park is expected to be completed in 2036. But parts of the park are already available to the public. When completed, it will be almost three times larger than Central Park.

WASTE TERMS

Sometimes people call the items they throw away trash or garbage. Sometimes they say rubbish or refuse. These words actually mean different things. *Trash* is the dry items people throw away. That includes items such as paper, boxes, and cans. *Garbage* is wet items. That includes food scraps and grass clippings. *Refuse* means both wet and dry items. *Rubbish* means just about everything discarded from both homes and businesses. *Municipal solid waste*, or *waste*, is another term for refuse.

Colored and labeled bins help people separate different types of waste.

Landfills that are not designed and operated properly can pollute the environment. New methods of waste disposal may provide a solution. New York City now buries some of its waste in nearby states. Some waste is sent to a power plant in New Jersey. The plant burns the waste to generate power. These operations have replaced Fresh Kills Landfill.

Major cities such as New York City produce a lot of waste each day. Waste solutions help keep cities clean.

They help cities get rid of waste efficiently. Residents may not always think about where their waste goes. But waste solutions are an important part of daily life.

TYPES OF WASTE

Today people produce more waste than ever before. In 2012 cities around the world threw away 1.4 billion tons (1.3 billion metric tons) of waste. Americans threw away approximately 258 million tons (234 million metric tons) of waste in 2014. That's an average of 4.6 pounds (2.1 kg) per

WHAT'S IN OUR GARBAGE?

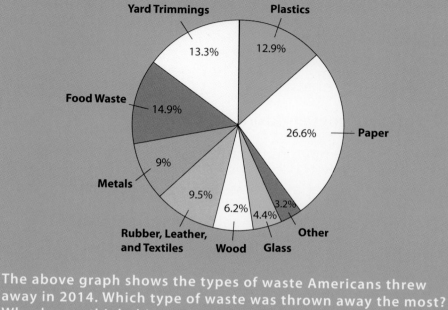

Yard Trimmings 13.3%
Plastics 12.9%
Food Waste 14.9%
Paper 26.6%
Metals 9%
Rubber, Leather, and Textiles 9.5%
Wood 6.2%
Glass 4.4%
Other 3.2%

The above graph shows the types of waste Americans threw away in 2014. Which type of waste was thrown away the most? Why do you think this was?

day per person. It is also nearly three times the amount that was thrown away in 1960.

Waste today contains a lot of plastic. Many plastic items are designed to be used once and then thrown away. These items include plastic trash bags, bottles, and eating utensils. Even many items that are designed to last are thrown away. Many people discard appliances rather than fix them. People throw away computers and cell phones when new versions come out.

Electronic devices that are thrown away are known as e-waste.

Most electronics should not go into landfills because they contain toxins such as lead and mercury. Many US states have mandatory recycling programs for electronics. But a lot of e-waste is exported to poor countries, where it poses health risks to residents.

PROBLEMS WITH WASTE

Waste that is not disposed of properly becomes litter. Litter can emit pollution as it decomposes. It can release harmful chemicals, such as ammonia. These chemicals pollute the land and water. For these reasons, litter can be dangerous to people and animals.

It is important for cities to manage waste properly. First the waste must be collected. Then it must be sorted. Different types of waste are handled differently. The last step in the process is to dispose of the waste. All waste is buried, incinerated, recycled, or composted.

STRAIGHT TO THE
SOURCE

The Puente Hills Landfill near Los Angeles, California, was the largest landfill in the United States before it closed in 2013. Journalist and author Edward Humes described the size of the landfill:

> Puente Hills has been the final resting place for the lion's share of Los Angeles County's ample daily flow of garbage for more than three decades—130 million tons [118 million metric tons] of it and counting.
>
> One hundred thirty million tons [118 million metric tons]: Such a number is hard to grasp. Here's one way to picture it: If Puente Hills were an elephant burial ground, its tonnage would represent about 15 million deceased [elephants]—equivalent to every living elephant on earth, times twenty. If it were an automobile burial ground, it could hold every car produced in America for the past fifteen years.
>
> Source: Edward Humes. *Garbology: Our Dirty Love Affair with Trash*. New York: Penguin, 2012. Print. 20.

What's the Big Idea?

Read the passage above carefully. What is the main idea? What details does the author use to support this idea?

BURYING WASTE

Historically, the most common way people have dealt with waste has been to bury it. The easiest burial method is to pile it in an open hole. This is called a dump. Dumps are usually located outside of large cities. Open dumps are still common in poor countries, such as India.

Leachate is a major problem in open dumps. Leachate is usually acidic. This makes it harmful to the environment and to human health. It soaks into the ground. It can also wash into nearby streams and rivers.

In the city of Goiânia, Brazil, waste from a truck is unloaded at a landfill.

GARBOLOGISTS

Waste pits near ancient cities and towns around the world contain things people used and threw away. These artifacts tell stories about how people lived long ago. In these waste heaps is a record of what clothes people wore, what tools they used, and what foods they ate. In the same way, modern landfills can be studied to learn more about modern society. Scientists called garbologists dig into landfills. They collect, sort, and catalog the garbage. Waste in modern landfills is well preserved because it decomposes at a slow rate. Garbologists have dug up whole steaks in modern landfills. These findings confirm that Americans throw away a lot of food.

From there, it can pollute groundwater and drinking water supplies.

SANITARY LANDFILL SCIENCE

In the mid-1900s, many cities replaced their dumps with landfills. A landfill is a place where waste is buried. Waste is covered by a layer of dirt each day. The layers help seal in the waste and prevent erosion. Modern landfills are lined with plastic to protect groundwater from leachate. They are called sanitary landfills.

Many countries have rules about where a landfill can be built and how it can operate. Engineers, geologists, and scientists first study the land. They look at the type of soil and underlying rock at the site. The rock should have as few cracks as possible. This helps prevent leachate from leaking into the groundwater.

Scientists also study the flow of water in the area. A landfill should not drain into rivers or wetlands. Scientists also consider the possible effects a landfill may have on wildlife. For example, the site should not bother nesting or migrating birds. Archaeologists may also be called in to see if the site has historical importance. Developers must avoid building landfills near schools, residential areas, and airports. Landfills often attract birds, which can interfere with airplanes during flight. Finally, the site must be large enough for the landfill. The largest landfills can cover more

Plastic liners and pipes are key parts of a sanitary landfill.

than 1,000 acres (400 ha) and rise taller than a 40-story building. If the site location passes inspection, the government grants a permit. It may take the government up to 10 years to issue a permit for a landfill. Then construction can begin.

The first step in the construction phase is to build access roads to the site. Then workers dig a large pit. They line the pit with clay and a layer of plastic. The plastic liner protects the ground from the waste and from leachate. Pipes are placed on top of the liner. These pipes collect and drain leachate into nearby holding ponds. The leachate may be treated on-site. This treatment involves using microorganisms such as bacteria to remove carbon and nitrogen from the waste. Or the leachate may be sent to a wastewater treatment plant for treatment. Modern landfills contain wells for monitoring groundwater. The wells are checked regularly to see if leachate is leaking.

Each day's waste is dumped into an area of the landfill called a cell. Bulldozers drive over the cell many times. This compacts the waste. Six inches (15 cm) of dirt is spread over the cell at the end of the day.

When waste decomposes in a landfill, it mainly produces methane and carbon dioxide. Methane can burn or explode under certain conditions. Gases collect in pockets deep in the landfill. Pipes are buried in the landfill. They bring the gas to the surface. Methane is then burned or collected. Burning, or flaring, converts

CLOSING A LANDFILL

Eventually a landfill will get too full or too high. Then it must be closed. A final cap is put over the top. The cap is a thick plastic liner. The cap is topped with two feet (0.6 m) of dirt. Then it is planted with grass. The grass helps keep the soil from eroding. Closed landfills have been used for golf courses, baseball fields, and parks. But closed landfills can continue to produce gas and leachate. They must be monitored for at least 30 years after closure to ensure they stay safe.

the methane to carbon dioxide. Collected methane can be turned into a fuel. It can also be used to generate electricity. Methane fuel can power cars and homes.

LANDFILL OPERATION

Most landfills are open every day. They are used mostly by city waste collectors and construction companies. Sometimes people bring their waste directly to a landfill. Attendants usually weigh the waste or count the number of truckloads. The customer then pays a fee based on the weight of the waste or the

Pipes transport methane gas out of a landfill into a separate plant, where it is burned for fuel.

number of truckloads. Customers can be individuals, companies, or waste collectors.

Landfills do not accept items that are hazardous to the health of people and the environment. Banned materials include paint, bleach, and batteries. Waste is considered hazardous if it could ignite or explode or if it contains chemicals that are poisonous. Many landfills have a household hazardous waste drop-off station for these items. From there, the items can be disposed of safely. Workers may recycle hazardous materials or incinerate them.

RUNNING OUT OF ROOM?

The amount of waste buried in US landfills has doubled within the last 50 years. Approximately 135 million tons (122 million metric tons) of waste were buried in the United States in 2012.

Today there are more than 1,500 landfills in the United States. Sanitary landfills keep air and liquid out. Water and air speed up the decomposition process. As a result, waste decomposes at a slow rate in sanitary landfills. This causes sanitary landfills to eventually fill up.

Most people do not want a landfill near where they live. For this reason, finding new spots to build landfills can be challenging. When landfills fill up, communities may explore new ways to dispose of waste.

STRAIGHT TO THE
SOURCE

In an essay, American author Wallace Stegner recalled the town dump when he was a boy living in Whitemud, Canada:

The town dump was our poetry and our history. We took it home with us by the wagonload, bringing back into town the things the town had used and thrown away. . . . If I were a sociologist anxious to study in detail the life of any community I would go very early to its refuse piles. For a community may be as well judged by what it throws away—what it has to throw away and what it chooses to—as by any other evidence. For whole civilizations we sometimes have no more of the poetry and little more of the history than this.

Source: Wallace Stegner. *Wolf Willow: A History, a Story, and a Memory of the Last Plains Frontier.* New York: Penguin, 2000. Print. 36.

Changing Minds

The author of this essay argues that the best place to learn about a city is at its dump or waste disposal site. Do you agree or disagree? Imagine your friend has a different opinion. Write a short essay trying to change your friend's mind. Include facts and details that support your reasons.

BURNING WASTE

Another way to dispose of waste is to burn it in a controlled manner. This occurs in a process called incineration. Incineration reduces large amounts of waste into a pile of ash. The ash is then recycled or moved to a landfill.

POLLUTION CONTROL

Many cities encouraged people to burn their waste in the early 1900s. People burned waste in barrels in their backyards. Businesses and factories burned their waste too. But burning waste causes pollution. It releases toxic

A waste-to-energy plant in Augsburg, Germany, burns garbage from the surrounding communities for fuel.

chemicals into the air, such as dioxin. Dioxin is linked to many health problems, including cancer. Burning waste also releases gases, including carbon dioxide. Carbon dioxide is a greenhouse gas. Greenhouse gases trap some of the sun's heat in the atmosphere. This warms the planet over time.

If not controlled properly, burning waste can create smog. Smog is smoke that contains microscopic particles. These particles cause air pollution. Smog can make breathing difficult. As a result, many cities banned backyard garbage burning. Cities began to build large furnaces called incinerators. Waste was collected throughout the city and brought to incinerators to be burned.

HOW DOES WASTE BURN?

Fire requires oxygen, fuel, and heat. In an incinerator, the fuel is waste. Waste is heated until it releases gases. The gases react with oxygen. This chemical reaction is called combustion. Combustion releases thermal energy and results in flames. The fire keeps burning as long as there is enough fuel and oxygen.

New clean air laws were passed in the 1970s. These laws required incinerators to limit the release of pollutants. Filters and scrubbers were installed in some incinerators. These tools clean gas in a flue, or chimney. They trap small particles and some gases. Incinerators not meeting the new regulations were forced to close. Today all modern incinerators are required to use the best available pollution control equipment.

THE POWER OF WASTE

When waste is burned, it produces heat. The heat can be used to produce electricity at special power plants. These plants are called waste-to-energy (WTE) plants.

First, trucks deliver waste to the plant. The waste may include food waste, plastics, glass, paper, and metals. Trucks dump the waste into a pit. Cranes then pick up the waste and drop it into a chute. From there, it moves to a furnace. The waste is burned, or combusted. Temperatures in the furnace can

At WTE plants, workers use cranes to pick up and move waste.

reach 1,560 degrees Fahrenheit (850°C). The high temperatures burn waste efficiently.

The combustion process produces heat, or thermal energy. That energy heats water in pipes. The water

evaporates and turns to steam. The steam turns a
turbine. A turbine looks like a big fan. When the steam
moves through the blades, the turbine spins. The
spinning turbine produces electricity. The electricity

WASTE-POWERED VEHICLES

Waste produces another type of energy called biogas. A special type of bacteria that doesn't need oxygen lives in landfills. The bacteria break down garbage. They turn the waste into biogas. The methane in biogas can be turned into a fuel called compressed natural gas (CNG). CNG can power vehicles. Methane in biogas also can be used to produce electricity. Each day, a typical landfill could produce enough electricity to fuel 1,200 electric cars. Garbage trucks can run on biogas. The trucks can collect the waste that would eventually become their own fuel.

travels through power lines to houses and businesses.

THE FUTURE OF WTE

Burning waste at a WTE plant reduces the volume of waste by up to 90 percent. Ash is left behind. Metals such as steel and iron are separated from the ash for recycling. The remaining ash is moved to a landfill or reused. Ash can be used as a material to build roads.

In 2015, 71 WTE plants plus four other

power plants burned waste in the United States. Those plants burned approximately 29 million tons (26 million metric tons) of waste per year. They produced nearly 14 billion kilowatt hours of electricity. That is enough to supply approximately 1.3 million US homes with electricity for one year.

MELTING WASTE

Researchers are working on a new way to make waste almost disappear. This process is called plasma gasification. Plasma is a substance that is similar to a gas. But unlike gas, it has charged particles. The particles move and create an electric current. In nature, lightning and stars are made of plasma. In the plasma gasification process, plasma torches heat waste at high temperatures. The waste doesn't burn. Instead, it turns to gas.

Shredded waste is loaded into a furnace. The waste is first heated to approximately 1,500 degrees Fahrenheit (800°C) and mixed with oxygen and steam.

The WTE plant in Vienna, Austria, is both a work of art and an efficient incinerator that supplies heat for more than 60,000 households.

This turns approximately 80 percent of the waste into gases. The gases include hydrogen and carbon monoxide. The gases are piped out and collected. They can be used as fuel. They can also be used to power a turbine and generate electricity.

After the gas is separated out, the remaining waste moves to another furnace. Plasma torches in the furnace heat the waste at 18,000 degrees Fahrenheit (9,982°C). That is almost as hot as lightning. At that temperature, the waste doesn't burn. Instead, it basically melts. The result is a small lump of shiny rock called slag. The slag can be used as a construction material.

This process reduces the volume of waste by 99 percent. Unlike burning waste, no ash is left over to be buried. The process has not been used on a large scale yet. But a demonstration gasification plant has been built in Tulsa, Oklahoma.

EXPLORE ONLINE

Chapter Three discusses different ways waste can be turned into energy. The website below provides a virtual tour of a WTE plant. What new information did you learn from this website?

ENERGY FROM WASTE
abdocorelibrary.com/providing-waste-solutions

RECYCLING AND COMPOSTING

Many modern cities are looking into ways to reduce the amount of waste headed for landfills. Recycling programs are one common way cities reduce waste. Some cities also offer citywide composting. In 2014 Americans recycled and composted more than 89 million tons (81 million metric tons) of trash.

Recycling trucks collect a community's recyclables and bring them to materials recovery facilities.

33

RECYCLING

Many things that are thrown away can be used again. Recycling is the process of collecting those items and making them into new products. Paper, cardboard, glass, metals, and plastic items can be recycled.

Many cities have recycling programs. San Francisco, California, leads the way in recycling efforts within the United States. Cities such as Copenhagen, Denmark, and Curitiba, Brazil, have high recycling rates as well.

The first step in the recycling process is to collect the items

Recyclables may be sorted by hand at a materials recovery facility.

that can be recycled. Some cities have drop-off centers. People bring their recyclables to these centers. Many cities send trucks to collect recyclables placed in bins outside homes. In some US states, stores that sell products in bottles and other recyclable containers charge customers an extra 5 to 15 cents as a deposit. People can return their empty bottles and containers to places called redemption centers. Then they get their deposit money back. These programs encourage recycling and reduce litter.

Collected items are sent to materials recovery facilities. The items are sorted by hand or by machine. Items that cannot be recycled are removed and disposed of properly. The rest are separated by category. Categories include metals, paper, and glass. Then the items are cleaned. They are sent to other facilities for processing. Processing involves breaking down items into their basic parts. Those parts can be used to make new things. For example, paper is often shredded and mixed with water and chemicals. This creates a mixture called pulp. The pulp is washed to remove inks, glues, and staples. The clean pulp can be used to make new paper products. Common household items that contain recycled materials include paper towels and aluminum cans.

COMPOSTING

Composting is a natural way to recycle organic materials. Organic waste materials include yard trimmings and food scraps. Composting is the breaking down of these materials in a controlled way.

RECYCLING RATES

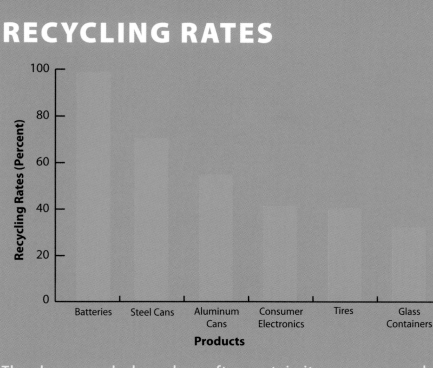

The above graph shows how often certain items were recycled in the United States in 2014. Why do you think some items were recycled more than others?

Some people compost in their backyards. Composting results in a product that can be used. Compost can be added to gardens and farms to improve soil. It returns nutrients to the soil. It also helps the soil stay moist longer.

Some cities have organic collection programs. Residents put organic waste into a bin. They place the bin on a curb or take it to a collection point.

At some composting facilities, machines line up organic waste in rows.

Compost collectors hired by the city pick up the waste. They take the waste to composting facilities.

In composting facilities, the materials are first sorted. Items that cannot be composted are removed and disposed of properly. The rest is put in big rows, piles, or special containers. Machines and large trucks help with all these tasks. Worms, ants, and beetles help break down bigger pieces. Then bacteria and fungi get to work. They use oxygen to decompose the materials. They produce carbon dioxide and heat in the process. In some cases, there are fans placed below the pile of waste. The fans blow air up through the pile. This helps aid the decomposition process.

THE FUTURE OF WASTE DISPOSAL

As the world's population grows, so does the world's waste. The more industrialized a country is, the more waste it produces. The countries that produce the most waste include the United States, China, Brazil, Japan, and Germany.

The world's annual waste production is expected to grow to 4 billion tons (3.6 billion metric tons) by 2100. Current research is focused on how to make recycling methods more effective. This could reduce the amount of waste generated globally.

Cities are also finding creative ways to encourage people to recycle. Artists in Houston, Texas, have turned recycling trucks into traveling works of art. The Art

AN OCEAN OF WASTE

As the amount of waste increases, so does pollution. A lot of waste ends up in the world's oceans. Waste washes into rivers and streams. Eventually, it reaches the sea. The United Nations estimates that approximately 7 million tons (6.4 million metric tons) of waste ends up in the seas each year. Most of that waste is plastic. The waste swirls into giant "patches" of garbage. One garbage patch in the South Pacific is estimated to be approximately 1 million square miles (2.6 million sq km) in size. The waste washes up on beaches. It kills seabirds, turtles, whales, and other marine animals that try to eat it or get tangled in it.

Recycle Truck project is designed to bring art into communities and spark interest in recycling.

Many cities are focusing on ways to reduce the amount of waste residents throw away. This is known as source reduction. Most cities charge a flat fee for waste collection. That means people pay the same amount whether they throw away a little or a lot. But some cities have adopted pay-as-you-throw

(PAYT) programs. Under these programs, people pay based on the amount of waste they produce. This encourages people to throw away less waste.

City engineers will need to develop new ways to handle the increasing amount of waste. This will involve designing better landfills and more efficient ways to turn waste into energy. New efforts to improve recycling will also help. Finally, cities can develop programs to encourage residents to throw less away. Advances in these areas will help cities around the world save resources and reduce pollution.

FURTHER EVIDENCE

Chapter Four discusses efforts to reduce waste through recycling and composting. What was one of the main points of this chapter? Watch the video at the website below. Does the information in the video support this main point? Or does it offer new information?

VISITING A RECYCLING PLANT
abdocorelibrary.com/providing-waste-solutions

FAST FACTS

- In 2012 cities around the world generated 1.4 billion tons (1.3 billion metric tons) of waste.

- In 2014 Americans threw away approximately 5 pounds (2.3 kg) of waste per person each day.

- The world's waste is expected to grow to 4 billion tons (3.6 billion metric tons) per year by 2100.

- Today there are more than 1,500 large landfills still in operation in the United States. Landfills produce methane and carbon dioxide gases. They also produce a liquid called leachate that can be harmful if not managed properly. Modern sanitary landfills are designed to treat and clean the leachate.

- Waste can be burned to produce electricity at waste-to-energy plants.

- Recycling takes used items that would otherwise be thrown away and turns them into new, useful items.

- Americans recycled and composted approximately 87 million tons (79 million metric tons) of waste in 2013.

- Composting turns grass clippings, food scraps, and other organic materials into a product that can be used to improve soil.

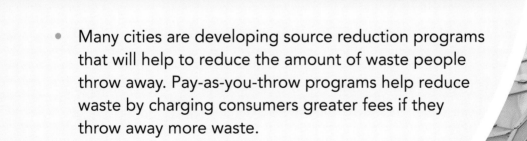

- Many cities are developing source reduction programs that will help to reduce the amount of waste people throw away. Pay-as-you-throw programs help reduce waste by charging consumers greater fees if they throw away more waste.

STOP AND THINK

Surprise Me

Chapter One of this book talks about the types of waste that get thrown away. After reading this chapter, what two or three facts about waste did you find most surprising? Write a few sentences about each fact. Why did you find each fact surprising?

Tell the Tale

Chapter Two discusses what can be learned about a community by studying its waste. Imagine that you are a garbologist who is studying your community's landfill. Write 200 words about what you might find there. What could the waste artifacts tell you about your community?

Say What?

Studying waste collection and disposal can mean learning a lot of new vocabulary. Find five words in this book you had never heard before. Use a dictionary to find out what they mean. Then write the meanings in your own words and use each word in a new sentence.